Michael

Saucy
Cookbook

British Broadcasting Corporation

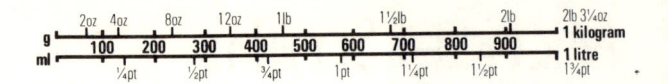

Published by the
British Broadcasting Corporation
35 Marylebone High Street
London W1M 4AA

ISBN 0 563 17511 7
First published 1978
© Michael Smith 1978

Cover photographs by Terry Hardman
Printed in England by
Belmont Press, Northampton

Contents

Introduction   5

Making a Perfect Basic Sauce   7

Rolled Butter (Beurre Manié)   10

White Sauces   11
The Perfect Rich White Sauce (Béchamel), Mornay Sauce, Onion Sauce, Caper Sauce, Mushroom Sauce, Quick Cream Curry Sauce, Shrimp Sauce
Sole Creams in Shrimp Sauce, Crunchy-topped Fish Pie   14

Velouté Sauces   16
Basic Velouté Sauce, Chicken Stock, Fish Stock, Sauce Suprême, Sauce Allemande, White Wine Sauce

Brown Sauces   19
Basic Brown Sauce, Bordelaise Sauce, Piquante Sauce
Duckling with Orange Sauce, Steak with Green Pepper Sauce   21

Hollandaise Sauce   23
Basic Hollandaise Sauce, Sauce Mousseline, Maltese Sauce, Sauce Foyot, Choron Sauce, Sauce Béarnaise
Avocado Pebble Mill   26

Other Savoury Sauces   28
Michael Smith's Bolognese Sauce, Tomato

Sauce, Bread Sauce, Curry Sauce, Cumberland Sauce
Chicken in Curry Mayonnaise — 33

Mayonnaise — 34
Basic Mayonnaise, Remoulade Sauce, Green Mayonnaise, Tartare Sauce, Gribiche Sauce, Cocktail Sauce, Aioli, Old English Salad Cream
Mimosa Eggs, Salmon or Smoked Haddock Mousse — 38

Salad Dressings or Sauces for Salads — 42
Basic Vinaigrette Sauce (French Dressing)
Avocado and Prawn Salad, Asparagus Vinaigrette — 46

Marinading and Macerating — 48
Basic Marinade
Marinated Kipper Fillets, Dobe of Beef (Dob'd Beef), Beef in Red Wine (Boeuf Bourguignonne) — 49
Michael Smith's Special Syrup for Fruit Salads — 53

Sweet Sauces — 54
Rich Apple Sauce, Apricot Sauce, Raspberry Sauce, Caramel Sauce, Custard Sauce, Orange Sauce, Hot Chocolate Sauce, Specially Rich Rum Sauce, Sour Cream Sauce
Vanilla Sponge Pudding, Old English Sherry Trifle — 58

Butters — 61
Hazelnut Butter, Cinnamon Butter, Garlic Butter, Herb Butter, Brandy or Rum Butter, Watercress Butter, Nut Butter (Beurre Noisette), Black Butter (Beurre Noir)

Introduction

In this book I will be covering some of the basic sauces, marinades and butters which I believe have slipped from favour and in many cases have disappeared altogether from our menus. If excellence in cooking is a priority in your life the basics are important, whether you are cooking for the family or for a special occasion.

Convenience foods are here to stay, and rightly so in a busy world. This means that creative cookery is fast becoming an enjoyable hobby and much of what I demonstrate on 'Grace and Flavour' is geared to helping viewers to enjoy the preparation as well as the final consumption of a particular dish. And whilst I feel that presentation and style of dishes is very important, using the best ingredients is imperative.

The right ingredients can *never* be an extravagance. There are still many who are frightened at the thought of using a carton of cream or 4 oz of butter in a recipe. But it is surely not extravagant if a carton of cream can extend 10 oz of chicken breast to feed eight people instead of four, as in the case of Chicken Creams (*More Grace and Flavour*, page 35). Similarly, if an extra 2 oz of unsalted Dutch or French butter makes a sauce velvety-smooth in texture and sublime in flavour, the small additional cost is well worth while.

The initial outlay on herbs and spices, wines and liqueurs can be high, but it has to be remembered that these are stock items and only a modicum is used at any one time. Friends who share your interest in good cooking may be only too happy to share the contents of a jar of one or more expensive spices. I have done this many times, particularly with saffron and other lesser-used 'exotics'.

Spices and herbs have been used since civilisation began to stimulate our olefactory senses through delicately perfumed dishes. It is the cook's art to stimulate and delight these senses by using his or her craft to lift the 'soul' of a dish.

Michael Smith

Making a Perfect Basic Sauce

There are many who will argue that there are only two basic sauces – brown and white. It is certainly true that these are the only two sauces where a roux (flour and butter) is the thickening agent. But today emulsion sauces are becoming popular as home cooks acquire finer techniques. (An emulsion sauce is when oil or fat is suspended in liquid, with egg yolk as the stabilising agent.) The two basic emulsion sauces are Mayonnaise (cold) and Hollandaise (hot).

There is also quite a comprehensive list of 'foreign' sauces such as Bread, Apple, Horseradish, Mint, Cumberland and Barbecue, to name but a few.

It is the above basic sauces which primarily concern us in this book as these form the basis of scores of other sauces served either separately or as an integral part of a dish.

A good sauce requires the following:
Excellent basic ingredients especially good quality butter and oil.
Patience slow, slow cooking, letting the flour cook out to give a bright (shiny) sauce, and allowing it to reduce to improve flavour and consistency.

A basic white sauce is composed of a roux plus milk (or in the case of Velouté Sauces, fish or chicken stock plus cream) and seasonings.

In the making of a white sauce a pale or blond roux is used. The butter is melted over a low heat, the flour stirred in then the roux is cooked, without allowing it to colour, for 5 minutes before any liquid is added.

When a brown sauce is being made, more heat is necessary and the roux is cooked until it is lightly browned and smells rather like baking bread. This is best made with two-thirds butter and one-third flour; most recipes call for equal quantities.

The liquids
For a white sauce milk is employed and is aromatised with onion and herbs. For Velouté Sauces and brown sauces good flavoursome chicken, veal, beef or fish stock is used.

Vegetables
The careful sweating (softening) and/or browning of vegetables is often neglected. Where a recipe calls for vegetables to be sweated this is done in melted butter and/or warm oil in a lidded pan over a low heat. Stir the contents to prevent any possible scorching or sticking. Cook slowly until the vegetables are soft.

When vegetables have to be browned – for a soup, sauce or casserole – this is done by first carefully letting the butter heat and colour (the butter will first foam and sizzle and then go 'quiet'). The vegetables are then added and evenly browned.

When a recipe asks you to cut your vegetables into even-sized cubes, sticks, shapes or pieces, the reasons are fivefold:
1. To achieve more facets for browning which will add more natural colour and flavour to your dish.
2. Each piece will take approximately the same

time to cook.
3. They are easier to manipulate (stir or shake) in the pan.
4. When flour is sprinkled over them for thickening purposes it is more evenly distributed and will brown more easily.
5. The vegetables will look more attractive.

Getting the right consistency
If a sauce is too thick add more liquid and reduce to the correct consistency or use Beurre Manié (page 10) to thicken it up.

To finish a sauce
All sauces should be strained through a hair sieve or conical strainer, any garnishes being added after straining.

To enrich a sauce
Bring the sauce to the boil, strain and immediately before serving beat in small pieces of softened (not melted) butter. This is called 'mounting' the sauce as the butter gives a lighter texture and lifts the sauce in volume.

To prevent a skin forming
Cover the surface of the sauce with a circle of well-buttered paper, which just fits. With a sweet sauce sprinkle with a fine coating of castor sugar.

To keep a sauce hot
With brown or white sauces stand the receptacle in another containing *just* simmering water. With an egg-based sauce stand the container over *warm* water as these sauces cannot be served hot.

Rolled Butter (Beurre Manié)

This cold roux, commonly known as Beurre Manié, is indispensable in any kitchen. It can be made up in quantity and kept in the fridge for as long as you would normally keep butter.

Most recipes suggest you use half butter and half flour. In my experience it is much better made with a higher butter content. So work 4 oz butter into a very soft state, then thoroughly blend in 3 oz flour. Store in a plastic container.

Whenever a soup, sauce, stew or gravy needs extra thickening, add small pieces of Beurre Manié and whisk or stir in. Allow time for each bit to do its thickening work before adding more.

To thicken one pint of sauce you will usually need plain flour in the following proportions: pouring sauce, 1 oz; coating sauce, $1\frac{1}{2}$ oz; binding sauce, 2 oz. To thicken brown soup you will rarely need more than $\frac{1}{2}$ oz of plain flour per pint. And most cream or velouté-type soups will require $\frac{3}{4}$ oz of plain flour per pint. Gravies, stews and casseroles, will not need more than $\frac{3}{4}$ oz of flour per pint.

When only a small amount of flour is needed for thickening it is easy to add Beurre Manié little by little until the liquid thickens.

The creative cook adjusts all the time to find the best combination of ingredients to achieve the correct consistency.

I have found that strengths of flour differ from brand to brand and readers will need to note the results they get from the brand they use and vary quantities if necessary.

White Sauces

The Perfect Rich White Sauce (Béchamel)

If you want a velvety-smooth delicately-aromatic creamy sauce, then here it is!

½ pint milk
¾ oz plain white flour
1 oz good butter
1 small piece onion
½-inch piece bay leaf
1 small sprig thyme (or tip of tsp dried)
1 small clove garlic, crushed
Salt and milled white pepper
1 good tbsp thick cream

Allow butter to just melt in small, heavy-bottomed pan. Stir in flour and gradually incorporate the milk (using a small balloon whisk, or a wooden spatula if a non-stick pan is used).

Add rest of ingredients, except cream. Simmer over lowest heat for 10 minutes, stirring from time to time. (You can use a modicum of ordinary white pepper instead of the freshly-milled white pepper but it is very strong. Milled black pepper tastes all right but leaves specks in the sauce.)

Strain into a clean basin, stir in cream and cover with a circle of buttered paper. Stand basin over a pan of simmering water to keep hot until required.

Mornay Sauce

To each ½ pint of Rich White Sauce add:

2 oz grated cheese (Gouda, Edam, Cheddar)	1 tsp lemon juice ½ tsp made-up mild French mustard

Serve with macaroni, cauliflower and poached fish.

Onion Sauce

To each ½ pint of Rich White Sauce add:

4 oz onion	1 tbsp water
1 oz butter	Nutmeg or mace

Slice the onion finely and soften in the butter and water in a lidded pan over a very low heat. Season with a modicum of nutmeg or mace. Put through sieve or blender.

Serve with roast lamb and with tiny boiled new potatoes.

Caper Sauce

To each ½ pint of Rich White Sauce add:

1 heaped tbsp capers	A little caper vinegar or lemon juice

Serve with roast lamb, brains, sweetbreads and poached fish.

Mushroom Sauce

To each ½ pint of Rich White Sauce add:

2 oz white button mushrooms	Mace or nutmeg
1 oz butter	1 tbsp dry madeira or sherry

Finely slice or chop the mushrooms and quickly fry them in the browned and foaming butter. Season with a modicum of mace or nutmeg and dry madeira or sherry. Serve with poached fish, eggs and macaroni (with cheese on top).

Quick Cream Curry Sauce

To each ½ pint of Rich White Sauce, add:

1 heaped tsp curry paste	1 tsp apricot jam
	1 tsp chutney

Press through a sieve before serving. Serve with boiled chicken, poached eggs, fish, cauliflower and celery.

Shrimp Sauce

To each ½ pint of Rich White Sauce, add:

4 oz shrimps or prawns	Salt
1 level tsp mild paprika	Lemon juice
	Brandy or whisky

Shell the frozen or fresh shrimps or prawns. Simmer shells (heads and all) in the Rich White Sauce for 20 minutes, together with the paprika. Strain, season with squeeze of lemon juice and a splash of brandy or whisky.

Add shrimps or prawns just before serving (they toughen up if allowed to boil in the sauce). Serve with poached fish, fish creams, cauliflower, poached eggs.

Sole Creams in Shrimp Sauce

10 oz raw sole when skinned and boned	Salt and pepper A touch of nutmeg Shrimp or Hollandaise Sauce
½ pint double cream	
2 eggs	

Before making the sole creams, make sure that you have a baking dish large enough to contain either castle pudding moulds or individual soufflé dishes. Failing this, small straight-sided coffee cups work very well. Alternatively the whole cream can be made in a ring mould. The quantity given will make eight creams in moulds which are 2½ inches in diameter. Butter the moulds well.

First prepare a Shrimp or Hollandaise Sauce (pages 13 and 23) for coating the creams.

Beat the eggs. Chill the cream in the refrigerator. Skin and bone the sole, put first through the fine blade of the mincer and then, with the beaten eggs, through a blender or Mouli, making as fine a purée as you can. Chill this well and then gradually beat the cream little by little into the purée, adding a little salt if it looks as though it is getting too thin. You will notice that the mixture seizes and thickens when you do this, but take care to be quite modest with the salt. Add a little pepper and nutmeg. When all the cream is incorporated, you should have a mixture which is just about dropping consistency.

Pre-heat the oven to gas mark 6, 400°F. Two-thirds fill the baking dish with hot water and place this on the centre shelf. Two-thirds fill the moulds, stand them in the water bath in the oven and bake for 25–30 minutes.

Have heated plates at the ready if you want the creams to be at their lightest. Turn out the creams and coat with either Shrimp or Hollandaise Sauce.

Crunchy-topped Fish Pie

2 lb cod or haddock fillet	*Topping*
1 pint Rich White Sauce	2 oz white breadcrumbs
4 oz peeled prawns	2 oz butter
2 hard-boiled eggs	Mashed potatoes
1 tbsp chives and/or parsley	

Make up the Rich White Sauce (page 11). Put the poached, skinned and flaked fish into a buttered ovenproof dish. Add the prawns, chopped hard-boiled eggs and finely chopped chives to the hot sauce and pour over the fish.

Fry the breadcrumbs in the butter until buttery crisp. Whip the potatoes with a goodly knob of butter and a big spoonful of cream (I use four jacket-baked potatoes scooped out, which are much tastier than boiled potatoes).

Fork a cushion of potatoes over the coated fish, sprinkle with the breadcrumbs and heat the pie through in the oven (gas mark 6, 400°F) until bubbling hot.

Velouté Sauces

These sauces are based on fish, chicken, veal and sometimes vegetable stock. They are thickened with a white roux and with the addition of cream. The most popular Velouté Sauce is made with chicken stock and is known as Sauce Suprême (page 17).

Basic Velouté Sauce

1½ oz flour
3 oz butter
1 pint strong chicken or fish stock

Melt the butter and gradually stir in the flour. Add the hot stock beating or whisking well until you have a smooth sauce. Simmer for 10 minutes and use appropriately.

Chicken Stock

To the skin and bones (not giblets) from a 2½ lb to 3 lb chicken or capon add:

2 carrots
1 onion
2/3 stalks celery
2 pints water
1 bay leaf
1 sprig celery
1 pinch thyme
6 peppercorns

Wash bones in cold water. Roughly chop carcase and vegetables. Put all ingredients into a pan and bring to the boil. Simmer for 1 hour. Keep stock well skimmed. Strain and keep cool until ready for use.

Fish Stock

To 2 lb of sole, turbot or bass bones add:

1 small onion	1 sprig parsley
1 carrot	1 bay leaf
1 celery stick	6 white peppercorns
2 oz mushroom stalks and peelings	½ bottle dry white wine
	2 pints cold water
Juice of ½ lemon	Salt

Wash bones well in cold water. Quarter the onion and roughly chop the carrot. Put all ingredients into a large pan and slowly bring to the boil. Simmer for 45 minutes. Strain and cool ready for use.

Add salt half way through cooking but only use a little as you may wish to reduce this stock later, thus increasing its saltiness.

Sauce Suprême

To each ¾ pint of Basic Velouté Sauce add:

¼ pint cream   Juice of ½ small lemon
Salt and pepper

Whisk in cream and lemon juice and season carefully. It is permissible to add a modicum of yellow colouring to this sauce. But take care that the brand you use is not flavoured. The colouring will enhance the creamy appearance of the sauce.

Serve with boiled chicken, pasta, and poached eggs.

Sauce Allemande

To each ¾ pint of Basic Velouté Sauce add:

¼ pint cream	Salt and pepper
2 egg yolks	Juice of ½ lemon

Beat the egg yolks into the cream and then whisk into the basic sauce. Add lemon juice and season carefully. Do not boil the sauce after the eggs have been added.

Serve with poached fish, poultry and eggs.

White Wine Sauce

½ pint fish stock	¼ pint thick cream
½ pint dry white wine	Salt
2 oz butter	Cayenne pepper
1 oz flour	Lemon juice

Mix together the fish stock (page 17) and white wine and reduce to ½ pint by boiling rapidly. Strain through muslin or a napkin.

Melt butter and gradually stir in flour. Beat in boiling stock. Simmer for 15 minutes. Stir in cream and season carefully.

If you want to glaze (brown) this sauce, beat two egg yolks with a little extra cream and whisk into the finished sauce. Do not let the sauce boil once the yolks are added.

Pour over the fish to be glazed and put under a spanking hot grill.

Brown Sauces

Basic Brown Sauce

2 tbsp olive oil
2 oz butter
1 small onion
1 4-inch carrot
1 celery stalk
2 oz field mushrooms, chopped
2 tsp tomato purée
1 chicken stock cube
2 oz flour
1 small bay leaf
1 good pinch of thyme
1 tsp red currant jelly
4 oz glass red wine or dry sherry
1½ pints water
Salt and freshly milled black pepper

Heat oil and butter until lightly smoking. Allow chopped carrot, celery and onion to gradually brown in this. Add mushrooms and continue to fry over a medium heat. Add tomato purée and, watching carefully as the purée burns easily, allow everything to take on a little more colour. Lower heat, add flour, stir well in and allow to brown stirring from time to time to prevent sticking.

Add herbs now (do not add earlier or they will burn and give a bitter taste). Add red currant jelly. Pour mixture into a clean dish whilst you pour into the frying pan the red wine or sherry. This will release any brown sediments on the bottom of the pan. Crumble in the stock cube. Return everything to the pan. Add the water, bring to the boil, adding a little (½ tsp) salt and pepper.

Simmer for 30 minutes, stirring to prevent sticking. Strain the sauce into a clean pan (you should have about 1 pint of sauce when it is finished). Adjust the seasoning with more salt if necessary. Cover with a circle of buttered paper and keep hot over simmering water until required.

This sauce can be frozen in small quantities and kept until needed.

Bordelaise Sauce

To each ½ pint of Basic Brown Sauce add:

1 small onion	1 oz butter or oil
2 oz mushrooms	

Fry the finely chopped onion and mushrooms in the butter or oil. This sauce classically is strained and contains a garnish of beef marrow. This refinement is entirely optional.

Serve with grilled steaks and chops, roast duckling, chicken or turkey.

Piquante Sauce

To each ½ pint of Basic Brown Sauce add:

4 tbsp red wine vinegar	1 tbsp gherkins
	1 tbsp parsley
1 tbsp shallot or onion	1 tbsp capers

Simmer the finely-chopped onion in the wine vinegar until the onion is soft. Add the finely chopped capers, gherkins and parsley.

Serve with grilled meats and deep-fried chicken.

Duckling with Orange Sauce

1 Duckling
½ tsp salt and black pepper
1 orange
1 oz butter

Sauce
1 orange
½ pint Basic Brown Sauce
2 tbsps brandy

Garnish
2 oranges, segmented
Watercress

Make a paste with the butter, finely grated rind of one orange, salt and pepper and rub this into the skin of the duckling. Roast at gas mark 5, 375°F, for 20 minutes to the pound. When the duckling is cooked, quarter or carve it and put into a warm serving dish.

Pour away all excess fat from the roasting tin. Pour in the brandy, blaze this, then add the brown sauce and juice of the two oranges. Reduce the sauce by boiling rapidly until it is bright and viscous. Season lightly if necessary. Strain into a smaller pan. Shred the orange rind and blanch in a little boiling water. Strain and add to the sauce.

Arrange orange segments over the cooked duckling and pour over the boiling sauce.

Decorate with bunches of crisp, lightly salted, watercress.

Steak with Green Pepper Sauce

4 fillet steaks
A knob of butter
2 tbsps olive oil
Salt and pepper
2 tbsps brandy
2 tbsps cream
$\frac{1}{4}$ pint Basic Brown Sauce
1 tbsp green peppercorns (in brine)

Trim the fillets of all fat and skin. Heat the oil in a frying pan, add the knob of butter. When the fat is hot and foaming fry the steaks to suit your taste. Season lightly after frying.

Remove steaks to a warm serving dish. Pour away all but one tablespoon of the pan juices. Pour in the brandy, ignite and whilst the alcohol is burning away add the Basic Brown Sauce and cream. Let the sauce bubble for a minute until all is smooth. (If it shows signs of being oily add a spoonful of water or stock.)

Season carefully with salt only. Strain into a little pan, re-heat, add the peppercorns and pour the hot sauce over the waiting steaks.

Hollandaise Sauce

Basic Hollandaise Sauce

2 tbsps white wine vinegar
3 tbsps water
1 small piece onion
6 peppercorns
1 small piece bay leaf
3 egg yolks
6 oz unsalted butter
Lemon juice
Salt and freshly-ground white pepper

Put the butter into a small pan and stand this in a warm place to melt and get quite hot. Put the wine vinegar, water, onion, peppercorns and bay leaf into a small pan and boil rapidly until the mixture is reduced to 1 tablespoon.

Now add two more tablespoons of water (you require the original quantity of liquid to extract the aromas in the first stage; you then need to replace some of the liquid which has evaporated).

Select a bowl which has a good round bottom and which will sit in the top of a pan of boiling water. Put the egg yolks into the bowl and strain the liquid on to them, stirring well with a tiny balloon whisk or spatula.

Arrange the bowl over the boiling water and whisk gently, but completely, taking care to see that the egg doesn't set on the sides of the bowl.

Continue whisking until the mixture is thick and the whisk leaves a definite trail, but stop before the eggs scramble! (Have a container of cold water to hand as a safety precaution. Dip the base of the bowl into the water to remove the residual heat quickly, thus avoiding any possibility of the egg over-cooking.)

Now stand the bowl on a folded damp cloth (this helps keep the bowl steady as you whisk). Whisk in a few drops only of the melted butter at first and as the sauce thickens add the butter more quickly until it is all incorporated (leave out the milky sediment which will have settled to the bottom of the pan whilst the butter has been slowly melting).

Adjust the seasoning, adding a little lemon juice and salt and pepper if you think it is needed. Squeeze little pieces of butter over the surface to prevent a crust forming. The butter can be whisked briskly into the sauce just before serving. Stand the sauce in a warm place until you are ready to use it.

As this is a warm sauce, it must not be kept where it is too hot or it will separate, so keep an eye on it. A good place to put it is on top of a plate which in turn is standing on top of a pan of hot, but not simmering, water.

Serve with any boiled or steamed vegetables, poached fish, hot fish mousses and soufflés, hot asparagus and hot artichokes.

Sauce Mousseline

To the Basic Hollandaise Sauce add:

$\frac{1}{3}$ pt cream

Half whip the cream before adding to the sauce.

Serve with any dish where Hollandaise Sauce could be served.

Maltese Sauce

Use the Basic Hollandaise Sauce but substitute orange juice for lemon juice and add 1 teaspoon of carefully grated orange rind and a hint of mace to the finished sauce.

Serve with any dish where Hollandaise Sauce could be served.

Sauce Foyot

To the Basic Hollandaise Sauce add:

1 tsp finely chopped or crushed garlic	1 tbsp chopped parsley
1 tbsp chopped tarragon	

Serve with poached or grilled fish, artichokes and grilled meats.

Choron Sauce

To the Basic Hollandaise Sauce add:

1 dsp mild tomato purée	1 dsp chopped tarragon

Serve with any dish where Hollandaise Sauce could be served.

Sauce Béarnaise

I put Sauce Béarnaise in this section for it is identical in make-up to Hollandaise Sauce but with a tarragon flavour. To make Sauce Béarnaise follow the recipe for Hollandaise but make the following changes:

At the 'reduction' stage, crumble into the liquid half a chicken stock cube (use Knorr or Maggi which are less potent than other brands). This is as good as the meat glaze called for in the traditional French recipe for Béarnaise.

Substitute tarragon vinegar for wine vinegar.

Finish the sauce with a dessertspoon each of chopped tarragon and/or parsley.

Don't add salt until the end as the stock cube may well suffice.

Serve with grilled fillet steak, baby lamb cutlets, grilled or deep-fried fish.

Avocado Pebble Mill

This is probably one of the richest starters you will ever taste, so serve with a very modest and plain main course and an even more modest pudding.

2 ripe avocado pears	$\frac{1}{2}$ pint Béarnaise Sauce
Lemon juice	4 lightly-boiled or
$\frac{1}{2}$ pint chicken stock	poached eggs
(from stock cube)	

First make up the Béarnaise Sauce (page 25) and put to keep warm.

Poach or lightly boil the eggs. Cut the avocado pears in half, remove the stone and rub the exposed surface with lemon juice.

Select a shallow pan just large enough to contain the pears face down. Bring the stock to the boil and pour over the pears in the pan. Heat through over minimum heat (approximately 5 minutes).

Arrange each pear in an individual dish. If you use boiled eggs (easier), shell them and pop an egg into each stone pit. Sprinkle over a little extra lemon juice for astringency and a little freshly-milled black pepper. Coat with Béarnaise Sauce and serve immediately with fingers of dry wholemeal toast. Eat the pears with a teaspoon.

Other Savoury Sauces

Michael Smith's Bolognese Sauce

¾ lb best stewing or rump steak
2 oz onion
3 tbsps olive oil
3 oz tomato purée
1 oz flour
½ pint red wine
½ pint stock (from stock cube)
1 large clove of garlic
Salt and freshly-ground black pepper

Strip the steak of fat and sinew (I always use rump which is a little more expensive but has an excellent flavour). In areas where fat-free mince is available this is also good for this dish. Put the meat through a mincer twice.

In a heavy-bottomed pan fry the finely chopped onions in the oil until golden brown. Gradually add the minced meat, stirring well over a good heat until the meat browns. Now reduce the heat and add the tomato purée, taking care to work it well in and see that it does not burn. Sprinkle the flour over and mix well in.

Now – and here is the secret of a good brown sauce – over a low heat gradually allow a crust to form on the bottom of the pan. This should take about 10 minutes, but watch it carefully.

Remove the mixture to a large dinner plate. Turn up the heat again and pour in the red wine. With a wooden spatula work all this crust into a sauce. When the bottom of the pan is quite clear, replace the meat mixture into the winey sauce, add the crushed and chopped garlic and the stock and simmer for 30 minutes. Season lightly, bearing in mind that the stock cube already contains salt.

Serve with any pasta.

Tomato Sauce

2 lbs tomatoes
1 tbsp tomato purée
1 small onion
1 clove garlic
2 rashers plain bacon
½ pint stock (from stock cube)
½ oz white flour
1 oz butter
¼ tsp grated lemon rind
¼ tsp powdered rosemary
1 tsp lemon juice
1 small glass medium sherry
1 tsp brown sugar
Salt and freshly-milled pepper

Heat butter in a heavy-bottomed pan. Fry strips of bacon and chopped onion until lightly browned. Stir in tomato purée (you could use ketchup), watching carefully as purée burns easily.

Stir in flour and add all seasonings (crush the garlic). Add sherry, stock, lemon juice, and the tomatoes, skinned and de-seeded.

Simmer for 20 minutes until sauce is bright or shiny. Press through hair sieve, correct consistency, adjusting with more stock. Salt and sugar to your taste.

Re-heat before serving.

If a creamy sauce is required, add ¼ pint double cream after the sieving stage.

Serve with poached and grilled fish, poultry, ravioli, gnocchi, canneloni, fish cakes and grilled sausage.

Bread Sauce

This sauce can be the dull stodgy stuff frequently served in restaurants in England, or the very refined sauce I give below:

½ pint milk
2 oz butter
1 small onion
½ clove garlic
1 bay leaf or a little nutmeg or 2 cloves
Salt and freshly-milled white pepper
3 oz fresh white breadcrumbs
¼ pint single cream
A little white stock or extra milk

Put the milk, butter, garlic, bay leaf (nutmeg or cloves) and onion into the top of a double saucepan and make the mixture as hot as possible. Add the breadcrumbs and let the sauce cook until it is quite thick and smooth. Pass the entire contents of the pan through a blender, Mouli or hair sieve.

Add the cream, adjust the seasoning, re-heat and serve.

If the sauce is too thick (this will depend on the kind of bread you use) thin it down with a little white stock or milk.

If the sauce has to be kept hot, return it to the double saucepan after sieving and cover with a circle of buttered paper to prevent a skin forming. Keep the water in the bottom pan hot.

Serve with roast chicken, turkey, grilled sausage and rissoles.

Curry Sauce

This is a basic curry sauce which can be adapted to all sorts of uses and can be served either hot or cold.

1 onion	4 cloves
1 heaped tsp curry powder	½ bay leaf
1 tsp tomato purée	1 crushed clove garlic
½ oz flour	2 tbsps brandy (optional)
¼ pint chicken stock	Salt and freshly-ground pepper
1 dsp apricot purée or jam	Oil for frying
1 dsp sultanas	

Chop the onion and fry in 2 tablespoons of oil until golden brown. Add the curry powder and cook for 1 minute, stirring well. Add the tomato purée and then the flour.

Reduce the heat and let a crust form on the bottom of the pan (this will give both colour and flavour to the sauce). Remove the mixture from the pan and swill the bottom with brandy or a little stock, incorporating any crust. Return the mixture to the pan and add the stock and other ingredients. Bring to the boil and simmer for 20 minutes.

Strain into a basin and leave to cool, covered with an oiled paper.

If you wish to use the sauce cold for a chicken mayonnaise dish or to use with cold poached fish, add half as much again of thick mayonnaise (page 34) and stir well in. If the sauce looks too thick, add a little lemon juice and a touch of cold water.

If you want a hot, creamy sauce for boiled

chicken with rice, or noisettes of veal, add ¼ pint double cream and bring the sauce back to the boil.

Cumberland Sauce

- 1 lb redcurrant jelly
- ¼ pint ruby port
- 3 oranges
- 3 lemons
- 1 level dsp dry mustard
- 1 small onion
- Salt
- Tip of tsp powdered mace
- 1 sherry glass cider vinegar

Using a potato peeler, remove the rind from all six pieces of fruit. Care must be taken to ensure that no white pith is taken off with the rind, as this is the bitter part of citrus fruits.

Collect the strips of rind together into manageable piles and with a very sharp, thin-spined knife shred the rind as finely as you possibly can – try to shred it as fine as a pin, for this will ensure that your sauce is good-looking and elegant. (Patience at this stage will pay dividends.)

Put the shredded peel into a pan and pour over enough water to cover it. Bring the contents of the pan to the boil and immediately pour into a strainer. Cool the peel under running cold water for a minute or so, then put on one side to drain.

Finely chop the onion. Squeeze and strain the juice of two of the oranges and two lemons. Bring this to the boil with all the remaining ingredients and simmer for 15 minutes over a low heat, stirring to ensure that the jelly melts evenly and doesn't burn. (Always use ruby port rather than tawny as this gives a good colour.)

Add the shredded rind and boil for a further 5 to 10 minutes until the sauce starts to thicken. Cool, then refrigerate until the sauce is somewhat jellied. Served chilled and do not strain.

Serve with cold roast meats, galantines, and terrines.

Chicken in Curry Mayonnaise

1 boiled capon or chicken

Sauce
½ pint mayonnaise
½ pint curry sauce

Garnish
8 oz flaked almonds
1 oz butter
Salt
1 tin apricot caps

Boil or steam the chicken, in the usual way. Reserve the stock for use in soups.

Cool, strip and bone the bird and cut the flesh into striplets or cut into serving-size pieces.

Mix the curry sauce (page 31) and mayonnaise (page 34) together, adjusting the consistency so that it just coats the chicken.

Pour sauce over the chicken pieces. Sprinkle with almonds which have been lightly browned in foaming butter, cooled and lightly salted.

Decorate with apricot caps (drained).

Mayonnaise

Basic Mayonnaise

½ pint nut oil
½ pint olive oil
6 egg yolks
1 tsp dry mustard
1 tbsp wine vinegar
Cold water
Salt and freshly-
 ground white pepper

Separate the eggs and put the yolks into a round-bottomed basin. This is essential as you need to collect and control the yolks within a small area. Add the salt, mustard and a little pepper and work these with a balloon whisk, or more laboriously with a wooden spoon, until they are really thick and sticky. (This recipe is not suitable for a blender.)

Have the oil in a jug; then by first using a teaspoon, add drops of oil to the egg mixture, whisking vigorously. Beat each drop well in before adding the next few drops. It is essential to take care in the early stages of mayonnaise making – if you are meticulous at the beginning, you will have no trouble later.

After the first tablespoonful or so of oil has been added you can start to add the oil more quickly – experience will teach you just when this can be done. As soon as the emulsion starts to reject the oil (this is quite different from curdling) add a little vinegar and beat until it is creamy again. Mayonnaise is curdled when the yolks and oil are flecked and liquid instead of creamy. If this happens you must start again with a single egg yolk and work the curdled mayonnaise into it drop by drop. Sometimes a tablespoon of boiling water added to the curdled mayonnaise will do the trick.

Keep the mayonnaise as stiff as your arm will allow! If you have a strong arm you will be able to make mayonnaise as thick as butter, which could be cut with a knife. If the mayonnaise is too thick thin it down with single cream, vinegar or cold water (or a combination of all three); water gives a blander result than vinegar, cream adds richness.

The finished mayonnaise can be flavoured with ketchup, sherry, lemon juice, brandy or Worcester sauce.

Store mayonnaise in a cool, but not cold, place. It does not keep indefinitely, but will be quite all right for four or five days. If it begins to look oily, just add a tablespoonful of boiling water and whisk until it is creamy again.

Remoulade Sauce (quick method)

To each ½ pint of Mayonnaise add:

1 heaped tbsp finely chopped piccalilli
1 dsp chopped parsley

Serve with deep-fried crumbed fillets of place or goujeons of sole.

Green Mayonnaise

To each ½ pint of Mayonnaise add:

1 large bunch watercress
1 tbsp parsley
1 tbsp chervil or chives
1 tbsp tarragon
Squeeze of lemon juice

Pick the watercress leaves and plunge into boiling salted water for 3–4 minutes. Run under cold water to cool. Drain very well pressing to remove all liquid. Blend this with the Mayonnaise (this is best done in a blender). Add the herbs and lemon juice.

Dried herbs will not do for this bright green sauce but 1 teaspoon of onion juice can be substituted for the chives or chevril.

Serve with cold fish pâtés, grilled or poached salmon, cold poached eggs.

Tartare Sauce

To each ½ pint of stiff Mayonnaise add:

1 dsp chopped capers	1 dsp parsley
1 dsp gherkins	Squeeze of lemon juice
1 dsp shallot or onion	Salt and pepper

Adjust consistency with water or thin cream if necessary. Only add salt and pepper if the sauce needs it for your taste.

Serve with grilled or deep-fried fish, fish cakes.

Gribiche Sauce

To each ½ pint of Tartare Sauce (above) add 1 finely chopped hard-boiled egg.

Serve as an alternative to Tartare Sauce.

Cocktail Sauce

To each ½ pint of stiff Mayonnaise add:

1 dsp tomato purée (or ketchup)	1 large tsp lemon juice
1 tsp Worcester sauce	1 large tsp brandy

Fold in a tablespoon of stiffly beaten cream for extra richness.

Use for dressing shrimps, prawns, and crab cocktails.

Aioli

Pronounce this sauce 'I-o-lee'.
To each ½ pint of stiff Mayonnaise add:

Lemon juice	8 cloves garlic

Pound the garlic to a paste. If you don't have a mortar and pestle, this can be done in a blender or by using the butt of a rolling pin.

Small spoonfuls of this sauce can be added at table to such soups as fish, tomato, celery and vegetable, giving a warming touch.

This garlic sauce can also be served with any raw vegetables as an appetizer or hors d'oeuvre. The raw vegetables, or crudités, are cut into attractive and manageable pieces and served in a large bowl of crushed ice (or even ice cubes and water) to keep them crisp and fresh.

The vegetables can be prepared the morning or day before a party and packed into plastic bags (keeping each vegetable separate). Chill but do not freeze.

Suggested vegetables are: carrot sticks; cauliflower florets; cucumber sticks (de-seeded but not peeled); whole radishes; fennel or celery sticks; tiny button mushrooms; baby new potatoes, cooked; green or red peppers, de-seeded and cut into strips; celeriac, cut into thin sticks.

Old English Salad Cream

1 tbsp flour
½ tbsp pepper
1 egg
4 tsps salad oil
1 tsp salt
4 tsps mustard
4 oz sugar
1 pint milk
½ pint white vinegar or ¼ pint brown vinegar

Mix all dry ingredients together, add oil and sugar. Beat the egg well into the milk and then gradually mix with the dry ingredients. Add vinegar slowly and then thicken by heating in a double boiler or in a bowl over a saucepan of boiling water, stirring all the time.

Bottle when cold.

Serve (as used to be the custom in England between the wars) with delicious cold poached salmon.

Mimosa Eggs

6 hard-boiled eggs
½ pint Mayonnaise
Lemon juice
A little cream
1 tbsp chopped chives or parsley
Watercress

Shell the eggs. Cut four of them in half lengthways and arrange in a serving dish. Cut the other two in half, remove the yolks and press the whites through a hair sieve.

Make a Basic Mayonnaise well spiked with lemon and mixed with a little cream to bring it to a coating consistency. Stir in the chives or parsley and coat the halved eggs.

Spoon small portions of the sieved egg whites between each egg and then press the yolks through a clean dry hair sieve letting the mixture 'rain' over the coated eggs. Add bunches of watercress for garnish.

Salmon or Smoked Haddock Mousse

1½ lb middle-cut Scotch salmon or smoked haddock
1 small onion
1 carrot
1 sprig dill weed or parsley
Water
Salt and peppercorns
½ pint Basic Mayonnaise
½ pint double cream

Juice of ½ a lemon
Salt and freshly ground white pepper

Aspic
Fish stock
1 oz gelatine

Garnish
Commercial aspic
Dry white wine
Tomato
Cucumber

Select a pan just large enough to hold the piece of salmon. For a piece as small as this there is little purpose in using a fish-kettle.

Wash and scale the fish and leave it ready to poach. Fill the pan with enough water to just cover the fish. (Stand a small oiled plate on the bottom of the pan to prevent the skin from sticking.)

Peel the onion and the carrot and cut them

into quarters. Add these to the water, together with the dill or parsley and a little salt. Bring the liquid to the boil and simmer for 10 minutes before lowering in the piece of salmon.

Poach the salmon for 20 minutes only, and leave it to cool in the poaching liquor. Remember that to poach means to cook so slowly that the water is only just moving.

When the fish is cool, lift out the salmon and skin it. Take away the dark 'band' down the spine, using a teaspoon to help you. Carefully remove every bone and then pound the fish flesh in a heavy basin (or in a mortar).

Put this pounded fish on one side whilst you make the Basic Mayonnaise (page 34) and aspic.

If you are using haddock, poach the haddock in slightly salted water acidulated with a little lemon juice and flavoured with a few parsley stalks, a bay leaf and a piece of onion. Drain, remove any skin and bone, and pound.

To make the aspic, first measure half a pint of fish stock; pour through a strainer into a pan and bring to the boil. Add the gelatine (this is double the usual amount of gelatine, as the aspic has to 'support' quite a lot of ingredients).

Arrange the bowl in a sink of running cold water, making sure that there is no chance of any of the water getting into the aspic! Stir from time to time to ensure even cooling; don't let it set.

Whip the cream until it just starts to ribbon but is not stiff.

Put the salmon into a large bowl and season with a little more salt, a modicum of freshly ground white pepper and a little lemon juice.

Beat in the mayonnaise and add more seasoning

if you feel it necessary. Pour in the cold, but not set, aspic and incorporate thoroughly. Fold in the half-whipped cream carefully but thoroughly.

Pour the mixture into a mould or soufflé dish – if you intend to unmould the mousse, the container should be lightly oiled and a circle of greaseproof paper fitted in the bottom. It is probably much simpler, however, to leave the mousse in its dish. Cover with foil, and put into the refrigerator to set.

Make up ½ pint of commercial aspic jelly with the normal amount of crystals asked for on the packet but using half dry white wine and half water.

Let the jelly cool, but not set, then run a thin layer over the top of the mousse and return it to the refrigerator to give the jelly time to set.

Stir the remaining aspic with a warm spoon to ensure that it doesn't suddenly set.

Decorate the mousse as you will. You can decorate the top quite professionally with sections of egg-white, blanched tarragon leaves or sprays of dill, quarters of unpeeled cucumber, strips of skinned and de-seeded tomato, olive rings, etc. Then very carefully float a little more jelly on the top to 'fix' the decoration. Put this again in the refrigerator. Finally, float the rest of aspic on to the top. If you follow this method of decorating, the pieces will not float away and leave you frustrated!

Serve the mousse with Sauce Mousseline (page 24) seasoned to taste with lemon juice and cream. Use water, not milk, to thin the mayonnaise down if necessary.

Salad Dressings or Sauces for Salads

Just when we in Britain fell from grace in this field and lost the host of ideas for dressing a 'grand sallat' given by the 17th-century diarist, John Evelyn, in his *Acetaria*, is not clear. But things are at last taking a turn for the better and bottled salad dressing is slowly disappearing to the back shelf, only to be used in cases of dire need.

A good dressing – be it a simple Vinaigrette, a rich French Mayonnaise, or a homely Old English Boiled Salad Cream – is the most attractive part of a salad.

The following are the basic requirements for any salad making. Your palate will dictate the combination which is preferable.

Bases
Oil, yoghurt, cream, sour cream, soft cheese, pulped avocado.

Acidulating agents
Red or white wine vinegar, citrus fruit juices, brandy, sherry.

Herbs, spices and aromatics (root herbs)
There was a time when herbs and spices were used abundantly in English cooking, particularly in the 16 and 17th centuries. It is often thought that they were employed to disguise tainted foods and there must have been times when this was the case. But there is evidence in old cookbooks

that herbs spices and aromatics were also used to enrich dishes and delight the palates of mediaeval gentlemen and their entourages.

Over-spicing and over-herbing is common today, usually because herbs and spices have been stored badly and for too long. Dried herbs should be kept in a cool dark place and should be used within twelve months (even then their efficacy has probably deteriorated drastically). If herbs and spices have lost their colour and look 'bleached' their usefulness is finished.

The following herbs and spices frequently appear in cookbooks:

Herbs: Basil, bay, chervil, dill, fennel (fronds or fern), marjoram, mints (all varieties: lemon, spearmint, peppermint), oregano, parsley, rosemary, sage, tarragon, thyme, watercress.

Spices: Allspice, cardamom, cinnamon, clove, curry(ies), ginger, malt, mustard(s), nutmeg, pepper (black, white, cayenne, paprika), saffron.

Aromatics: Garlic, onions, scallions, shallots, leeks, chives, vanilla.

Never buy dried parsley, it is the one herb which must be used fresh. Do think about growing your own herbs, not only are the rewards great, but it is cheaper and very satisfying.

If you are not accustomed to using dried herbs I suggest you try the powdered type first. These are much easier to use than the leaf type, as you can almost gauge what scent they are going to give off by smelling at the bottle. The leaf type takes longer to infuse.

Sweeteners
Scented honeys, brown or white sugar, treacle and syrups, ketchup, liqueurs, fruit juices.

Remember that cane sugar is sweeter than beet sugar and that different brown sugars can be used to vary the flavour of syrups, cakes, puddings and sauces at no extra cost. (I'd like to make the point here that brown sugar ought never be used to sweeten coffee as it changes the flavour of the beverage too drastically.)

Oils
Olive, arachide (peanut), walnut, almond, sesame-seed, sunflower seed, corn (not so good for salads).

Mustards
French, English, German, mild, strong, with or without seeds.

Bouquet garnis
Bouquet garnis are easily obtainable in most shops and may be substituted in recipes where a mixture of herbs is called for.

A controversial point on salad bowls
I always wash my wooden salad bowl and it is still with me with only one minor unimportant crack after twenty years.

If a bowl is used regularly there may be no need to wash it; but I have been served many a salad from a wooden bowl which has smelled very rancid and has tainted the freshly made salad.

An enamel, stainless steel, ceramic or glass bowl is as adequate as a wooden bowl (the dressing doesn't cling to the sides and aesthetically wood may be more pleasing, but these are moot points.)

What is important is to wash your lettuce in an abundance of cold water; shake it dry and then pat dry with a clean towel or kitchen paper. Always tear the leaves, never cut them and never dress a green salad until the last minute or the leaves will be soggy.

You should add just enough dressing so that each leaf glistens and no dressing is left in the bottom of the bowl.

It is not advisable to keep green salads for re-use once they are dressed.

Basic Vinaigrette Sauce (French Dressing)

6 tbsps olive oil
$\frac{1}{2}$ tsp mustard
2 tbsps red or white wine vinegar
$\frac{1}{4}$ tsp castor sugar
Salt and freshly-milled pepper
1 clove garlic (optional)

Finely chop the garlic. Put all the ingredients into a screw-topped jar and shake until completely blended.

Vinaigrette Sauce keeps almost indefinitely in a screw-top jar. Do not add garlic and herbs until ready for use.

Avocado and Prawn Salad

3 large ripe avocado
  pears
Juice of ½ lemon
4 oz shelled prawns
2 sticks celery
¼ cucumber
1 cup French Dressing
1 clove garlic
1 tbsp chopped parsley
1 tbsp chives or
  spring onion
1 tsp grated lemon
  rind

Garnish
2 tomatoes
4 lemon segments
1 hard-boiled egg
Parsley

Cut two of the pears in half, remove the stone and rub the surface of the flesh with lemon juice. Wrap each half of pear in cling film and refrigerate until ready for use. Peel the third pear, cut in half, pit and then dice the flesh putting it immediately into the French Dressing (page 45) to prevent discolouration. Add the rest of the ingedients to the dressing. Mix well and put to chill.

To serve, pile the diced filling into each half shell. Decorate with the tomato, egg and lemon segments. Sprinkle with parsley and stand the pears in avocado dishes or on saucers. Eat with a stainless steel teaspoon.

Asparagus Vinaigrette

This is served as an hors d'oeuvres.

Fresh asparagus   French Dressing

Cook the asparagus for 20 minutes in boiling salted water, then plunge into cold water. Drain well on a clean tea towel as asparagus tends to hold water.

Make up a French Dressing (page 45) adjusting the quantitiy to your requirements but allowing approximately 1 tablespoonful of dressing per six stalks of asparagus.

Arrange the asparagus in a dish and sprinkle the tips with the dressing.

Marinading and Macerating

Marinading

The marinade, as we know it today, is a method of delicately seasoning and tenderising meat, fish, poultry and game before cooking it. It is the acid content of the marinade that helps to break down any toughness in the fibre.

Before the days of refrigeration, wine (being a disinfectant) was used by the French to help preserve their meat. There came a point when they realised that not only did it help to preserve, but, if they used some of the marinade in the actual cooking of the dish, it made for interesting eating. Eventually, the chef of the house started to add other ingredients in the form of vegetables, herbs, spices and aromatics and such prize dishes as Coq au Vin and Civet de Lièvre were created.

The more expensive cuts of British meat are a great deal tenderer and more flavoursome than continental meat and does not need marinating. But the cheaper cuts of meat can be improved using a marinade. It takes time to get used to new flavours and I have always been cautious as to how long I marinate my meats. Always marinate in an enamel pot or glass bowl or dish and cover it closely using a lid, cling film or foil.

Don't be surprised if you get raised eyebrows when your guests sample the marinated meat. It is in the meat that the different flavour really shows. The sauce made from the marinade will taste more or less the same as any wine sauce.

Basic Marinade

To make 1 pint of marinade.

1 large onion
1 large carrot
1 large clove garlic
1 teacup red or dry white wine
½ teacup red or white wine vinegar
½ teacup olive oil
1 bay leaf
1 dozen peppercorns
Salt

Very thinly slice the onion and carrot. Lightly salt and pepper the meat or fish. Place the meat in your dish and mix with the vegetables, crushed and chopped garlic, crushed bay leaf and peppercorns. In a pan warm the oil, vinegar and wine. Pour over the rest of the ingredients.

Leave meat to marinate in the refrigerator for one or two days, turning and basting every three or four hours.

Marinated Kipper Fillets

4 uncooked kippers (2 pairs)

Marinade
1 level tbsp bland nut-oil
1 tbsp red or white wine vinegar
1 tbsp onion
1 dsp parsley

Garnish
Rye bread fingers
Chopped parsley

Using your fingers and a very sharp, thin-bladed knife, carefully skin and fillet the kippers. Cut each fillet diagonally into six or seven strips, following the natural grain of the fish.

Finely chop the onion and chop the fresh parsley. Put into a screw-top jar and shake until blended. Put the strips of kippers into the marinade, cover with foil, chill and marinate for at least 3 hours. You could also marinate the kippers in French Dressing (page 45).

Serve with a little extra freshly chopped parsley on top and buttered rye bread fingers.

Dobe of Beef (Dob'd Beef)

This is based on a Tudor recipe.

2 lb best rump steak	ground black pepper
4 oz fat pork or bacon	
2 carrots	*Garnish*
2 onions	4 oz button
2 cloves garlic	mushrooms
½ stick celery	8 artichoke bottoms
½ tsp thyme	(tinned)
½ tsp marjoram	4 cooked new potatoes
6 cloves	1 cooked carrot
2 oz butter	1 tbsp parsley
1 pint strong ale or port	2 oz butter
1 oz flour	Lemon segments
1 tsp grated orange rind	
½ pint strong stock	
Salt and freshly-	

Trim the meat of the skin and fat and cut into 1-inch cubes. Cut the bacon or pork into ¼-inch dice. Cut all the vegetables into ½-inch dice. Put the meat and vegetables, together with the garlic and orange rind, into a dish and cover with the ale or port.

Sprinkle with the freshly chopped herbs (if dried ones are used, these should be tied in a bag and put into the dobe with the vegetables). Leave the meat to marinate for 4 or 5 hours, overnight, or longer.

Drain the meat cubes and the vegetables, retaining the liquor. Melt the 2 oz of butter in a heavy-bottomed pan and when it has acquired a nice nutty flavour, brown the bacon in it, add the meat cubes and fry at a high temperature until the meat is sealed. This will be best done if you fry a little at a time.

Add the vegetables and the dried herbs if these are being used. Sprinkle with the flour, stir well in and cover with the marinade and the stock. Lightly salt and pepper, remembering that the sauce will be well reduced and therefore strong.

Transfer all the contents of the pan to an earthenware casserole and cover tightly, sealing the lid with a flour and water paste. Cook in the oven at gas mark 3, 275°F, for 5 hours. The finished dish should be a strongly flavoured, cohered mass.

For the garnish, cut and dice all the vegetables and toss them in the butter until they are thoroughly heated through. Season lightly. Drain and arrange attractively on top of the dobe just before serving.

Sprinkle with freshly chopped parsley and serve with the lemon segments in a side dish.

Plain riced potatoes are perfect with a rich dobe – a potato ricer (masher) is a piece of equipment well worth having.

Beef in Red Wine (Boeuf Bourguignonne)

2 lb rump or braising steak	3 cloves garlic
Red wine marinade	4 oz button mushrooms
½ bottle red wine	1 oz butter
2 tbsps olive oil	1 bay leaf
8 oz button onions	1 sprig parsley
12 baby carrots	1 sprig thyme
8 oz bacon	Salt and freshly milled pepper
1 oz flour	

Cut the beef into sticks ½ inch by 1½ inches. Marinate in the Basic Marinade (page 49) made with red wine. Leave overnight.

Drain and pat dry the meat, retaining the liquid.

Cut the bacon in one thick slice then cut into sticks. Use whole baby carrots or cut larger carrots into even sticks.

Heat the oil and brown the bacon, then the carrots and then the onions, removing each to an ovenproof casserole as they are browned.

Now brown the beef, a little at a time, sprinkling with the flour and adding more oil if necessary. The oil will need to be smoking before each addition.

Bring the vegetables and meat together in the casserole, cover with the marinade and wine (making approximately 1 pint of liquid), season with the garlic, herbs, salt and pepper. Cover and cook in the oven, gas mark 3, 275°F, for 2½ hours to 3 hours. Quickly fry the white button mushrooms in 1 oz butter and add just before serving.

Sprinkle liberally with chopped parsley.

Macerating

This is when fruits are soaked in liqueurs, wines or spirits to enhance their flavour.

It is a touch of luxury to soak fruits for fritters before dipping them in batter, ie, bananas in rum, apple rings in Maraschino, pineapple sticks in Kirsch and apricots in Amaretto. For fruit salads soak strawberries, raspberries and currants in Dubonnet.

For a delicious red fruit bowl soak the fruit in spirits or use the following recipe:

Michael Smith's Special Syrup for Fruit Salads

2 navel oranges
2 lemons
1 lime
1 sherry glass Kirsch,
   Akvavit or gin

8 oz castor sugar
½ pint water

Remove the rind from the citrus fruits with a potato peeler. Shred very finely. (You will not need to use the flesh or juice.)

Put rind, sugar and water into a pan. Simmer until a light syrupy consistency. Cool and add the liqueur. Chill until required.

Spoon over any fresh fruits just before serving.

The juice from the citrus fruits may be used elsewhere or, if you are making a fresh fruit salad, the salad fruits may be soaked in the juices before pouring the Special Syrup over at the last minute.

Sweet Sauces

Rich Apple Sauce

This recipe restores apple sauce to its former Tudor glory.

4 Cox's apples
1 tbsp castor sugar
1 oz unsalted butter
1 oz ground almonds (optional)
2 tbsps water (or orange juice)

Peel, quarter, core and slice the apples. Melt the butter and sugar in the water or juice. Add the apples.

Simmer in a lidded pan until soft. Stir in the almonds and either blend, or press through a hair-sieve.

Re-heat carefully or serve cold with roast pork, duckling or sausages.

Apricot Sauce

4 oz can apricot caps or 2 tbsps apricot jam
1 oz sugar
2 tbsps Grand Marnier, Kirsch or Amaretto

Drain the apricots, retaining 2 tablespoons of the syrup. Put all ingredients together in a pan. Simmer for 5 minutes. Blend or press through a hair-sieve.

If you want a tangier sauce add 1 tablespoon of lemon juice instead of the liqueurs.

Serve, either hot or cold, with hot sponge puddings, baked bananas, rice pudding and ice cream.

Raspberry Sauce

8 oz fresh or frozen raspberries
Juice of 1 lemon
3 oz castor sugar
2 tbsps gin or water

Bring all the ingredients to the boil over a very low heat. Simmer gently for 5 minutes and then very gently press the contents through a fine sieve, applying only a minimum of pressure to the fruit so that the sauce remains clear. If you wish you can serve the sauce without sieving.

Serve, either hot or cold, over pineapple, melon, sponge pudding (particularly chocolate pudding) ice creams and melbas.

Caramel Sauce

3 oz castor sugar
3 tbsps warm water
$\frac{1}{4}$ pint half-whipped double cream

Put sugar into aluminium pan (not enamel lined as the heat will crack the enamel). Allow sugar to caramelise slowly.

Cover your hand with a cloth and pour in the water (it will splutter and splash). Stir and allow to boil until syrupy. Cool, then stir in the whipped cream. Chill well.

Serve with caramelled pears or oranges, sponge pudding and ice cream.

Custard Sauce

1 pint milk (or half milk, half cream)
5 eggs
1 tsp cornflour
1 vanilla pod (or 1 tsp vanilla essence)
$1\frac{1}{2}$ oz castor sugar

Bring the milk to the boil, together with the vanilla pod, or essence. Mix the sugar with the cornflour, add the eggs gradually and beat the mixture well until it is smooth. Remove the vanilla pod from the saucepan and pour the boiling milk on to the egg mixture, stirring all the time.

Rinse out the pan, leaving a film of cold water in the bottom. Return the custard to the pan and stir with a wooden spoon over a low heat until it is thick. Plunge the bottom of the pan into a basin of cold water to remove any residual heat which might curdle the custard. Leave to cool.

Orange Sauce

½ pint orange juice (bottled, tinned or fresh)
1 tsp orange rind
1 oz castor sugar
1½ oz unsalted butter
1 oz plain white flour
¼ pint double cream

Melt butter, stir in flour, gradually add orange juice, allow to boil. Add sugar to taste and orange rind, simmer for 5 minutes. Add cream (do not use milk as this will curdle), bring to boil again and serve.

If serving cold, sprinkle surface with castor sugar to prevent skin forming.

Serve, hot or cold, with pies and puddings.

Hot Chocolate Sauce

3½ oz bitter chocolate
⅛ pint water
1 tsp vanilla essence
2 egg yolks
1 oz castor sugar
½ oz unsalted butter

Break chocolate into pieces and put in basin over boiling water together with sugar, essence, water and butter. Stir occasionally and allow to get quite hot. Remove basin from water and whisk in the two egg yolks.

If you want a cold sauce, leave to cool and if too thick whisk in a little water to slacken the consistency.

Serve with profiterôles, gâteau, ice cream, sponge puddings.

Specially Rich Rum Sauce

½ pint sweet white wine   2 oz castor sugar
3 tbsps Jamaica rum   Rind of 1 lemon
5 egg yolks

Cream the egg yolks and sugar until every granule of sugar has dissolved. Remove the rind of the lemon with a potato peeler or with a sharp knife, patiently shred this as fine as hair. Add to the egg yolks and stir in the wine and rum.

Arrange the basin over a pan of boiling water, making sure the water is in contact with the bottom of the basin. Whisk the sauce slowly, but continuously until it is as thick as double cream. Remove from the heat and continue whisking until the heat has diminished somewhat.

Keep the sauce warm over a pan of hot, but not boiling water. This time the water must not be in contact with the bottom of the basin.

Ideal with Christmas Pudding, vanilla sponge, a special apple pie or with ice cream.

Sour Cream Sauce

½ pint sour cream
2 oz castor sugar
1 small lemon
¼ tsp nutmeg
¼ tsp cinnamon
¼ pint double cream

Grate the rind of the lemon and stir into sour cream. Add the sugar, nutmeg and cinnamon. Whip the double cream and using a draining spoon fold in the sour cream mixture. Chill well.

Good with hot and cold fruit pies and puddings.

Vanilla Sponge Pudding

2 eggs
Unsalted butter
Castor sugar
Self-raising flour
2 tsps cold water

Weigh the eggs and use the same amount of butter, sugar and flour, (i.e., if the eggs weight 4 oz, use 4 oz butter, 4 oz sugar and 4 oz flour). Have the butter at room temperature, add the sugar and beat until every granule of sugar has disappeared. Add 1 teaspoonful of the flour and beat in well.

Beat the eggs with the cold water and gradually beat them into the creamed butter and sugar. Now deftly and thoroughly fold in the rest of the flour.

Spoon into a buttered pudding basin and cover with a circle of buttered foil that is big enough to give room for the pudding to rise.

Make sure the foil is well sealed round the brim of the basin so that no steam, which would make the top of the pudding wet, can get in. Have the steamer ready on the stove so that it is good and hot, ready to give the mixture its initial 'push into space'!

Steam for 1½ to 1¾ hours. Remember to top up the steamer with boiling water.

When serving, carefully remove the foil, run a knife around the sides of the basin and invert on to a warm serving dish.

Old English Sherry Trifle

Custard Sauce
Base
2 7-inch fatless sponge cakes or 1 packet small sponge cakes
1 lb apricot purée, apricot jam, or quince jelly
¼ bottle medium dry sherry

Topping
1 pint double cream
4 oz glacé cherries
4 oz blanched or toasted almonds
2 oz each crystallised apricots, crystallised pears or Carlsbad plums
2 oz crystallised chestnuts
4 oz ratafia biscuits
Angelica leaves

Use good quality sponge cakes. First make up the Custard Sauce (page 55). Split the sponge cakes in half across their middles; liberally spread them with purée, jam or jelly, sandwich them together and cut into 1-inch fingers. Arrange these in a shallow trifle dish, about 12 inches across the top and about 3 inches deep.

Sprinkle the sponge fingers with plenty of sherry and pour the waiting custard over them. Cool the trifle base completely. (If the bowl is glass, wipe away any condensation from the sides, as this will look unsightly when the trifle is cold.)

Prepare all the topping ingredients – the actual quantities will depend on the area of trifle to be covered and this is bound to vary slightly.

Cut the crystallised apricots or pears and chestnuts and Carlsbad plums into attractive quarters. Cut long spikes of angelica. Empty the packet of ratafias to free them from biscuit crumbs. Make sure that the blanched or toasted almonds are cold or they will melt the cream. Put each topping ready on a separate plate.

Whip the cream until it just stands in peaks but doesn't look as though it will be cheese at any minute! Spread a thick layer over the trifle. Decorate at will with the other topping ingredients.

You may like to make a fresh fruit trifle and in this case use fresh fruits only for decoration and stick them into the bed of whipped cream at the last moment so that the juices do not draw and spoil the look of the trifle. A purée of fruit can replace the jam in the sponge cakes. Particularly suitable fruits to use are strawberries or raspberries and fresh apricots. If you are using raspberries use Kirsch instead of sherry.

Butters

Savoury and sweet butters can bring great variety to your menus, remembering that they can be used in sandwich-making to give that little extra interest (see *Grace and Flavour*, page 29).

Try warming Eccles cakes, splitting them open and sliding in a disc of hazelnut or cinnamon butter, or toast slices of Sally Lunn (*More Grace and Flavour*, page 52) and spread with nutmeg or lemon butter, watercress butter is excellent on top of poached trout or as a spread in chicken sandwiches. Garlic butter is used to make hot crisp garlic bread (see page 62).

Hazelnut Butter

4 oz unsalted butter
2 oz toasted hazelnuts
1 tsp brown sugar

Cream butter and sugar. Beat in the finely crushed nuts, form into roll.

Cut into $\frac{1}{2}$ inch discs for topping grilled steaks, chops and fish.

Cinnamon Butter

4 oz unsalted butter
2 oz brown sugar
1 tsp powdered cinnamon
1 tbsp rum (optional)

Cream butter and sugar. Beat in the cinnamon and rum. Form into roll and use as previous recipe.

Garlic Butter

4 oz butter	Salt and freshly-ground white pepper
4 cloves garlic	
1 tbsp lemon juice	1 dash tabasco sauce

Cream the butter, add the crushed garlic, season to taste with lemon juice, salt and tabasco. Form into a roll, wrap in greaseproof paper and refrigerate.

Use for topping grilled steaks, chops and fish.

To make garlic bread, cut a French stick diagonally into inch-thick pieces (not cutting right through so that the stick holds together). Slide discs of garlic butter between each slice, wrap the bread in foil and heat through in the oven, gas mark 6, 400°F, for 10–15 minutes. Serve hot with the foil just folded back.

Herb Butter

4 oz butter	1 tsp basil
1 tsp parsley	1 tsp chives
1 tsp fennel fronds	$\frac{1}{2}$ crushed clove garlic
1 tsp chervil	Lemon juice
	Salt and pepper

Use freshly picked and chopped herbs. Cream the butter, beat in the garlic and herbs, season to taste with lemon juice, salt and pepper. Form into a roll and refrigerate.

Use as for Garlic Butter (make herb bread in the same way as garlic bread).

Brandy or Rum Butter

4 oz unsalted butter
4 oz castor sugar
4 tbsps brandy or rum
1 tsp lemon or orange juice
½ tsp lemon or orange rind
1 tbsp boiling water

Cut the butter into 1-inch cubes and put with the sugar and lemon rind into a basin. Beat until creamy, add the boiling water and continue to beat until every grain of sugar has been dissolved. Add the lemon juice and brandy and beat well in.

Put into lidded wax cartons and store in the refrigerator until ready for use.

This butter can safely be made two or three weeks in advance and should by no means be restricted to use on Christmas pudding.

I use white sugar and lemon for brandy butter, but brown sugar and orange for rum butter.

Brandy or Rum Butter is good served with hot pies and sponge puddings.

Watercress Butter

1 bunch watercress
2 oz butter
1 tsp lemon juice
1 pinch castor sugar
Salt and pepper

Use fresh, crisp watercress. Laboriously pick all the leaves from the stalks, then either put all the ingredients into a blender or pound with the butt of a rolling pin in a metal basin. Rub the finished butter through a hair sieve and form into a roll.

Nut Butter (Beurre Noisette)

4 oz butter

Melt the butter in a pan and let it foam. At the moment it begins to give off an almondy nutty flavour, pour immediately over grilled fish or poached eggs.

Black Butter (Beurre Noir)

4 oz butter	½ tsp cracked white
Juice of ½ lemon	(or black)
Salt	peppercorns

Swirl butter round in heavy bottomed pan until it passes the nut butter stage (see above). Do not allow the butter to burn, season to taste. Add lemon juice, to arrest the browning process.